LET'S SHARE OUR FEELINGS

WRITTEN AND ILLUSTRATED
BY
TERI RIDER

**Academic
Communication
Associates**

P.O. Box 4279
Oceanside, CA 92052-4279

**Academic
Communication
Associates**

P. O. Box 4279
Oceanside, CA 92052-4279
WEB: http://www.acadcom.com
E-Mail: acom@acadcom.com
Telephone Order Line: (888) 758-9558
Fax: (760) 758-1604
Printed in the United States of America
International Standard Book Number: 0-930951-18-2

Table of Contents

Introduction

Learning to express feelings is essential for the development of effective social interactions. Many children, however, have difficulty expressing their feelings or relating to the feelings of others. Some children are reluctant to talk about their feelings because of concerns about how others will react. Other children express feelings freely, but do so in a manner that causes their peers to react negatively to their behavior.

Communicating feelings is often difficult for children with communicative disorders. In many cases, these children have not acquired the vocabulary necessary to describe how they feel. They may also need to develop strategies for conveying feelings in a socially appropriate manner.

Although many teachers encourage children to share how they feel, activities designed to facilitate the expression of feelings are often not included in the educational curriculum. This book includes practical activities to help children develop an awareness of their feelings and to help them share those feelings. Children are also given opportunities to explore how their own feelings differ from those of others.

As students participate in the activities in this volume, they are presented with situations relevant to problems commonly encountered by young children. The short stories and problem situations can be used to stimulate group discussions on a variety of topics. These discussions provide opportunities for students to share their feelings and to listen to the feelings shared by others.

The activities in this volume were developed primarily for children between 5 and 11 years of age. They can be used in regular classrooms or in special education programs. The activities will be especially useful in programs for children with communicative disorders.

Learning to Express Feelings

As children develop proficiency in using language, they learn the "rules" governing how and when to express feelings. These rules vary depending on the context of the situation, the topic of conversation, and the social roles of the participants in the interaction.

During their social interactions, children learn that their own needs and feelings are often different from those of others in their environment. Children become aware that they cannot alway get what they want and that they must adapt to the needs and feelings of others.

Often feelings can be expressed in a variety of ways. Speech, hand gestures, facial expressions, and even periods of silence can be used to convey how one is feeling. One can convey anger, for example, by shouting loudly, by stomping out of the room, or by expressing concerns in a calm voice.

To express feelings effectively, one must become sensitive to the listener as an individual who also has needs and feelings. Children need to develop flexibility in how they express feelings so that they can adapt to the various situations that they encounter in their everyday activities.

Organization of This Book

Part 1 of this book includes short stories in which the story characters experience a variety of emotions. The stories can be read by the teacher or by the student. Each story is accompanied by an illustration. The story and the illustration may be reproduced for use with individual students.

A worksheet is included for each story. This worksheet has a variety of questions relating to the feelings of the story characters. Students are asked to talk about the feelings of the characters and to describe their own feelings when similar situations are encountered. The situations presented in the worksheet activities are relevant to problems commonly encountered by young children and can be used to generate group discussions.

The individual worksheets in Part 2 are designed to promote the understanding of specific concepts related to the expression of feelings. Students are given practice in classification, matching, and in the descriptive uses of language.

Part 3 includes three different types of drawing activities designed to strengthen students' understanding of specific concepts. Students are asked to create "doodles" showing specific feelings, to draw situations that evoke these feelings, and to draw themselves in situations where the target feelings are being experienced. These pages can be reproduced for use in creating student workbooks.

The activities in this volume can be presented by classroom teachers, speech-language pathologists, and special education teachers working in a variety of educational settings. All of the story picture pages and worksheets may be reproduced for use with students in your classroom.

Considering Individual Differences

When presenting the activities in this volume, it is important to consider cultural differences in how language is used to express feelings. What is judged to be an appropriate expression of feelings in one culture may be viewed as rude or unacceptable within another culture.

The materials in this volume should be adapted, as necessary, to meet the needs of individual students. This book can be used in conjunction with other published resources or with materials developed by the teacher. It is important to create an environment that will motivate students to become active participants in the learning process.

Part 1

Stories About Feelings

Thirty short stories are included in this section. Each story is presented on a picture poster with large text. The short story is also included on the worksheet that follows the picture poster. Read the story to the student or have the student read it independently. After the story has been presented, ask the questions listed on the worksheet. Space is included for recording the student's responses. All of the pages in this section may be reproduced for use with individual students.

Chelsea and Her Bunnies

Chelsea's mother gave her some stuffed bunnies for her birthday. Chelsea loved her stuffed bunnies. She had names for them and took them everywhere with her.

One day she lost one of her stuffed bunnies. She looked everywhere for it. Her favorite stuffed bunny was gone.

Activity 1- Chelsea and Her Bunnies

Student:_________________________________ Date:______________

Chelsea's mother gave her some stuffed bunnies for her birthday. Chelsea loved her stuffed bunnies. She had names for them and took them everywhere with her.

One day she lost one of her stuffed bunnies. She looked everywhere for it. Her favorite stuffed bunny was gone.

1. How did Chelsea feel about her bunnies?

____

____

____

2. How do you think Chelsea felt when she lost one of her bunnies?

____

____

____

3. What would you say if your friend was feeling bad after losing something special?

____

____

____

4. Do you think she would let her friends play with her bunnies?

____

____

____

5. Have you ever lost anything? How did you feel?

6. How would you feel if you found something that you had lost?

Far Away Places

Elmo always played by himself. He had a very good imagination. He imagined that he was exploring places far away. Sometimes he would paint pictures of these places and pin them to his wall. His sisters and brothers would tease him and call him names. He was very different from everyone else in his family.

It made Elmo sad when his family made fun of him. His parents rarely had time to talk to him, so he didn't share his thoughts with them. Elmo liked it better in the far away places he made up in his mind. Most of the time he sat in his room imagining that he was far away from home.

Activity 2- Far Away Places

Student:_________________________________   Date:______________

Elmo always played by himself. He had a very good imagination. He imagined that he was exploring places far away. Sometimes he would paint pictures of these places and pin them to his wall. His sisters and brothers would tease him and call him names. He was very different from everyone else in his family.

It made Elmo sad when his family made fun of him. His parents rarely had time to talk to him, so he didn't share his thoughts with them. Elmo liked it better in the far away places he made up in his mind. Most of the time he sat in his room imagining that he was far away from home.

1. Do you think Elmo felt happy or sad most of the time? Why?

____

____

____

2. Why did Elmo feel sad when his family made fun of him?

____

____

____

3. Do you think Elmo had many friends? Why do you feel this way?

____

____

____

4. Would you like to be friends with someone like Elmo? Why?

____

____

____

5. Do you know anyone like Elmo? What is this person like?

____

____

____

6. Can you think of something that is very special about Elmo?

____

____

____

7. How do you feel when someone makes fun of your ideas or creations?

____

____

____

8. How would you feel if people in your family made fun of you?

____

____

____

Joshua's Bad Mood

One day Joshua got mad at Markie when they were playing football. He pushed Markie down on the ground and walked away mad. Joshua had been in a bad mood all day. Markie was confused by Joshua's anger. They were good friends and usually didn't fight.

Activity 3- Joshua's Bad Mood

Student:_________________________________ Date:_______________

One day Joshua got mad at Markie when they were playing football. He pushed Markie down on the ground and walked away mad. Joshua had been in a bad mood all day. Markie was confused by Joshua's anger. They were good friends and usually didn't fight.

1. How did Markie feel when Joshua pushed him down?

____

____

____

2. Why do you think Joshua was in a bad mood?

____

____

____

3. Have you ever been in a bad mood? Why?

____

____

____

4. Have you ever done something you were sorry for later? What happened?

____

____

____

5. What can you do to change your mood when something is bothering you?

____

____

____

6. What would you say if a friend of yours was in a bad mood?

____

____

____

Twins

Ashley and Danielle are twins. They look almost exactly alike. Danielle is a little taller than Ashley. Ashley has more freckles. Ashley likes to pretend that she is Danielle, and Danielle likes to pretend that she is Ashley.

Their favorite thing to do is to play their "let's pretend" trick. They think it is very funny when people get them mixed up. Most people don't know which one is Ashley and which one is Danielle.

One day, they played their trick on the lady across the street. When she found out Ashley was pretending to be Danielle, her face turned red!

Activity 4- Twins

Student:_________________________________   Date:_______________

Ashley and Danielle are twins. They look almost exactly alike. Danielle is a little taller than Ashley. Ashley has more freckles. Ashley likes to pretend that she is Danielle, and Danielle likes to pretend that she is Ashley.

Their favorite thing to do is to play their "let's pretend" trick. They think it is very funny when people get them mixed up. Most people don't know which one is Ashley and which one is Danielle.

One day, they played their trick on the lady across the street. When she found out Ashley was pretending to be Danielle, her face turned red!

1. How do the twins play their "let's pretend" trick?

____

____

____

2. How do the twins feel when they trick someone?

____

____

____

3. How do you think the lady felt when they played their trick on her?

____

____

____

4. Should the twins play their trick on other people? Why do you feel this way?

____

____

____

5. Do you think they are having fun or trying to be mean? Why?

____

____

____

6. Have you ever played a trick on someone? How did the person feel?

____

____

____

At the Front of the Class

Charles liked school, but sometimes got nervous when
the teacher called on him to answer a question. One day he
was called up to the chalkboard to solve a math problem.
His stomach started to hurt and his hands started to shake.
He was afraid he would give the wrong answer.

Activity 5- At the Front of the Class

Student:________________________________   Date:______________

Charles liked school, but sometimes got nervous when the teacher called on him to answer a question. One day he was called up to the chalkboard to solve a math problem. His stomach started to hurt and his hands started to shake. He was afraid he would give the wrong answer.

1. Why did Charles' stomach hurt and why did his hands shake?

____

____

____

2. How would Charles feel if he gave the wrong answer?

____

____

____

3. What did Charles think would happen if he gave the wrong answer?

____

____

____

4. How would he feel if he gave the right answer?

____

____

____

5. What might make Charles feel better about going up in front of the class?

____

____

____

6. Have you ever been afraid to answer a question from your teacher when you were in front of the class? Why?

____

____

____

Will Anyone Help Amanda?

Sometimes Amanda had trouble doing her
homework. Her mom was usually too busy to help
her. When she asked her dad for help, he said that
he didn't have time. Nobody ever seemed to have
time to help Amanda.

Activity 6- Will Anyone Help Amanda?

Student:_________________________________   Date:______________

Sometimes Amanda had trouble doing her homework. Her mom was usually too busy to help her. When she asked her dad for help, he said that he didn't have time. Nobody ever seemed to have time to help Amanda.

1. How did Amanda feel when her parents would not help her?

____

____

____

2. Should Amanda tell her parents how she feels when they don't help her?

____

____

____

3. Who else could Amanda ask for help?

____

____

____

4. Why do you think Amanda needed help?

____

____

____

5. If Amanda felt like she wasn't smart, what would you say to her to make
her feel better about herself?

____

____

____

6. Have you ever felt like you weren't very smart? Why did you feel that way?

____

____

____

Henry Can Swim

Henry was invited to a swimming party. He wanted very much to go, but he didn't know how to swim. Henry was afraid of the water. Henry really wanted to learn how to swim and went to the swimming party anyway.

Activity 7- Henry Can Swim

Student:_________________________________   Date:______________

Henry was invited to a swimming party. He wanted very much to go, but he didn't know how to swim. Henry was afraid of the water. Henry really wanted to learn how to swim and went to the swimming party anyway.

1. How did Henry feel about the water?

   ____

   ____

   ____

2. If Henry tries hard enough, do you think he will be able to learn how to swim?

   ____

   ____

   ____

3. How do you think Henry will feel if he learns to swim?

   ____

   ____

   ____

4. How would you feel if everyone was swimming and you didn't know how to swim?

   ____

   ____

   ____

5. Have you ever been afraid to learn something new?

____

____

____

6. How do you feel when you do well learning something new?

____

____

____

The Baby Bird

Valerie found a baby bird that had fallen from it's nest. Valerie couldn't put the baby bird back into the nest because the nest was high in a tree. She decided to take the bird home. Valerie hoped she could feed the baby bird until it was strong enough to fly away on it's own.

Valerie spent a lot of time taking care of the baby bird. In a few weeks, it was ready to fly. Valerie had grown very fond of the baby bird and wanted to keep it for a pet. She knew she should set it free. She took it back to where she found it and let it go.

Activity 8- The Baby Bird

Student:_________________________________ Date:_____________

Valerie found a baby bird that had fallen from it's nest. Valerie couldn't put the baby bird back into the nest because the nest was high in a tree. She decided to take the bird home. Valerie hoped she could feed the baby bird until it was strong enough to fly away on it's own.

Valerie spent a lot of time taking care of the baby bird. In a few weeks, it was ready to fly. Valerie had grown very fond of the baby bird and wanted to keep it for a pet. She knew she should set it free. She took it back to where she found it and let it go.

1. How did Valerie feel when she found the baby bird?

    ____

    ____

    ____

2. Why did Valerie feel that she should take care of the baby bird?

    ____

    ____

    ____

3. What might have happened to the baby bird if she hadn't taken it home with her?

    ____

    ____

    ____

4. How did Valerie feel when she thought about setting the bird free?

____
28
____

____

5. Have you ever found an animal or bird and wanted to keep it for a pet? How did you feel when you found it?

____

____

____

The Grocery Store

Amber was in the grocery store with her mom. The store was crowded and Amber's mom was in a hurry. Amber was looking around at all the pretty things in the store. When she turned around, she didn't see her mother anywhere. Amber looked up and down the aisles but couldn't find her mom.

Activity 9- The Grocery Store

Student:_________________________________   Date:_______________

Amber was in the grocery store with her mom. The store was crowded and Amber's mom was in a hurry. Amber was looking around at all the pretty things in the store. When she turned around, she didn't see her mother anywhere. Amber looked up and down the aisles but couldn't find her mom.

1. How do you think Amber's mom felt shopping in a crowded store?

____

____

____

2. How do you think Amber felt when she couldn't find her mom?

____

____

____

3. What should Amber do to find her mom?

____

____

____

4. How do you think Amber's mom felt when she noticed that Amber wasn't with her?

____

____

____

5. How do you think they both felt when they finally found each other?

____

____

____

6. Have you ever gotten lost in a store? What did you do and how did you feel?

____

____

____

Alex and the Mouse

Alex traded his lunch to Billy for a pet mouse. Alex knew his parents didn't want him to have pets, so he hid the mouse under his bed.

Alex's mom found the mouse a few weeks later when she went to clean his room. Alex was asked why he had brought a mouse home without letting his parents know about it. Alex started to yell because he wanted to keep his pet. His mother told him that he couldn't keep it.

Activity 10- Alex and the Mouse

Student:_________________________________ Date:______________

Alex traded his lunch to Billy for a pet mouse. Alex knew his parents didn't want him to have pets, so he hid the mouse under his bed.

Alex's mom found the mouse a few weeks later when she went to clean his room. Alex was asked why he had brought a mouse home without letting his parents know about it. Alex started to yell because he wanted to keep his pet. His mother told him that he couldn't keep it.

1. How did Alex feel when he got the mouse from his friend?

____

____

____

2. How do you think Alex's parents felt when they found out he had been hiding the mouse?

____

____

____

3. Why do you think Alex's parents didn't want him to have a pet?

____

____

____

4. What do you think Alex's parents would have said if he had asked nicely for permission to get a pet?

____

____

____

5. How did Alex feel about having to get rid of his pet mouse?

____

____

____

6. How did Alex's parents feel when Alex argued with them?

____

____

____

7. How do you think Alex should have behaved when his mother found the mouse?

____

____

____

8. How would you feel if your mother or father told you that you couldn't keep a pet? What would you say?

____

____

____

Eric Doesn't Like to Talk

Eric sat in the back of the class hoping the teacher wouldn't ask him to read or talk. He had trouble moving his mouth when he talked. Sometimes he didn't say the words right. Some of his classmates laughed at him when he spoke.

Eric was trying hard to learn to speak better. It was very difficult for him.

Activity 11- Eric Doesn't Like to Talk

Student:_________________________________ Date:_______________

Eric sat in the back of the class hoping the teacher wouldn't ask him to read or talk. He had trouble moving his mouth when he talked. Sometimes he didn't say the words right. Some of his classmates laughed at him when he spoke.

Eric was trying hard to learn to speak better. It was very difficult for him.

1. How did Eric feel when the other kids laughed at the way he talked?

____

____

____

2. Have you ever known anyone who had trouble speaking clearly?

____

____

____

3. What did you say to this person when you couldn't understand what was being said?

____

____

____

4. How would you feel if your classmates laughed at the way a friend of yours talked?

____

____

____

5. How could you help someone like Eric?

____

____

____

6. If someone has difficulty speaking, does it mean that he or she is not as smart as most other people?

____

____

____

7. Do other kids ever make fun of you? How do you feel?

____

____

____

8. What would you say to someone who made fun of you?

____

____

____

The New Kid

Ryan was the new kid in class. He came from a different country and didn't speak English very well. Many of the kids teased him and said mean things. Ryan wanted to make new friends, but he was very shy. Nobody played with him.

Activity 12- The New Kid

Student:_______________________________   Date:_______________

Ryan was the new kid in class. He came from a different country and didn't speak English very well. Many of the kids teased him and said mean things. Ryan wanted to make new friends, but he was very shy. Nobody played with him.

1. Would you want to be friends with Ryan?

____

____

____

2. How do you think Ryan felt when the other kids teased him?

____

____

____

3. Would you have teased Ryan?

____

____

____

4. If you were Ryan's friend, what would you say to the other kids?

____

____

____

5. What would you say to Ryan when the other kids teased him?

____

____

____

6. What do you think Ryan should do if the other kids don't stop teasing him?

____

____

____

7. Have you ever known someone from another country who didn't speak English very well? How did you feel when you listened to this person speak?

____

____

____

Susie and the Softball Team

Susie liked to play softball. She was a very good player. There were only boys on the neighborhood team. They played every day after school. Susie decided to ask if she could play. Some of the boys wanted her to play. Most of the boys didn't want a girl on the team.

Activity 13- Susie and the Softball Team

Student:_________________________________ Date:_______________

Susie liked to play softball. She was a very good player. There were only boys on the neighborhood team. They played every day after school. Susie decided to ask if she could play. Some of the boys wanted her to play. Most of the boys didn't want a girl on the team.

1. What might Susie say to get the boys to let her play?

____

____

____

2. How would Susie feel if the boys decided to let her play?

____

____

____

3. Would some of the boys be mad if the team captain decided to let Susie play?

____

____

____

4. How would the boys feel if Susie became the best player on their team?

____

____

____

5. How would Susie feel if the team decided not to let her play?

____

____

____

6. Have you ever been told that you couldn't play on a team when you really
wanted to play? How did you feel?

____

____

____

Becky's Big Brother

Becky's big brother, Brad, was her best friend. He always did nice things and helped her with homework. After Brad graduated from high school, he went to college and had to move away.

Brad came home every month to visit, but Becky missed him badly.

Activity 14- Becky's Big Brother

Student:_________________________________   Date:_______________

Copyright © 1992 by Academic Communication Associates. This worksheet may be reproduced.

Becky's big brother, Brad, was her best friend. He always did nice things and helped her with homework. After Brad graduated from high school, he went to college and had to move away.

Brad came home every month to visit, but Becky missed him badly.

1. How do you think Brad felt when he was helping Becky?

____

____

____

2. How did Becky feel when Brad moved away?

____

____

____

3. How do you think Brad felt when he was away from home?

____

____

____

4. What can Becky do so that she doesn't miss Brad so much?

____

____

____

5. Has someone you really care for ever moved away? How did that make you feel?

____

____

____

6. Do you think that Becky and Brad can still be best friends even though they are living in different cities.

____

____

____

Sandy's Goldfish

Sandy had a pet goldfish. She took good care of her goldfish and fed him every day. One morning when she went to feed him, he was floating at the top of the fish bowl. Sandy's goldfish was dead.

Activity 15- Sandy's Goldfish

Student:________________________________   Date:______________

Sandy had a pet goldfish. She took good care of her goldfish and fed him every day. One morning when she went to feed him, he was floating at the top of the fish bowl. Sandy's goldfish was dead.

1. How do you think Sandy felt when her goldfish died?

____

____

____

2. What could you say to help Sandy feel better?

____

____

____

3. Should Sandy get a new pet? Why?

____

____

____

4. Do you think the new pet would make Sandy feel better?

____

____

____

5. Have you ever lost a pet? How did you feel?

____

____

____

6. Is it okay to be sad and miss a pet when it dies?

____

____

____

Miguel Liked School

Miguel liked school. He did well learning most things, but had trouble with spelling. Sometimes the teacher would explain things that Miguel just didn't understand. Miguel was afraid to tell the teacher when he had trouble understanding things. He didn't want her to think he was stupid.

Activity 16- Miguel Liked School

Student:_________________________________   Date:_______________

Miguel liked school. He did well learning most things, but had trouble with spelling. Sometimes the teacher would explain things that Miguel just didn't understand. Miguel was afraid to tell the teacher when he had trouble understanding things. He didn't want her to think he was stupid.

1. Why did Miguel feel dumb?

____

____

____

2. Should he ask the teacher for help after school so the other kids won't find out about his problem?

____

____

____

3. Do you think Miguel worried about what the other kids in his class thought about him?

____

____

____

4. How do you think Miguel feels about himself?

____

____

____

5. Have you ever had trouble understanding something? How did you feel?

____

52

____

____

6. What did you do when it was hard to learn something?

____

____

____

Belinda Bragged

Belinda always wore new clothes to school and always had new toys. She brought something new to school every day. She would brag to the other kids that she had better things than they did. She was always showing off.

Activity 17- Belinda Bragged

Student:_________________________________ Date:_______________

Belinda always wore new clothes to school and always had new toys. She brought something new to school every day. She would brag to the other kids that she had better things than they did. She was always showing off.

1. Why do you think Belinda liked to brag?

   ____

   ____

   ____

2. How do you think Belinda felt when she was bragging?

   ____

   ____

   ____

3. How did the other kids feel when Belinda bragged?

   ____

   ____

   ____

4. How would you feel if Belinda was always bragging to you?

   ____

   ____

   ____

5. What would you say to Belinda if she was bragging?

____

____

____

6. How do you feel when you get something new?

____

____

____

Manny Was Helpful

Manny liked to be helpful. He was always helping his teacher pass out papers and books. He always helped his parents by doing his chores at home. He also liked to help his friends with their homework and with special projects. He even helped his neighbors by doing small jobs for them.

Activity 18- Manny was Helpful

Student:_________________________________ Date:_______________

Manny liked to be helpful. He was always helping his teacher pass out papers and books. He always helped his parents by doing his chores at home. He also liked to help his friends with their homework and with special projects. He even helped his neighbors by doing small jobs for them.

1. Do you think Manny was happy being helpful?

____

____

____

2. How do friends like Manny make you feel?

____

____

____

3. How does it make you feel when you are helpful?

____

____

____

4. How would you feel if you were given the Student of the Week award for being helpful?

____

____

____

5. How do your friends feel when you help them with something?

____

____

____

6. How do you feel when someone helps you?

____

____

____

Rosie's Broken Bear

Rosie accidentally pulled the ear off of her stuffed bear. She only had one stuffed bear and liked to play with it. Rosie cried and cried. Then her big sister, Sherry, came home. Sherry picked up a needle and thread. Then she sewed the ear back on Rosie's bear for her.

Activity 19- Rosie's Broken Bear

Student:_________________________________   Date:_______________

Rosie accidentally pulled the ear off of her stuffed bear. She only had one stuffed bear and liked to play with it. Rosie cried and cried. Then her big sister, Sherry, came home. Sherry picked up a needle and thread. Then she sewed the ear back on Rosie's bear for her.

1. Why did Rosie cry?

____

____

____

2. Why did her big sister sew the ear back on Rosie's bear?

____

____

____

3. How did Rosie feel when the ear came off the bear?

____

____

____

4. How do you think Sherry felt when Rosie cried?

____

____

____

5. Did it make Rosie feel better to have her sister fix her bear?

____
61
____

____

6. Have you ever broken one of your favorite toys? How did you feel?

____

____

____

Tommy's Little Brother

Tommy liked to play football. He played football with his friends almost every day. His little brother, Ricky, always wanted to play with him. Ricky loved football but could not catch the ball. Tommy didn't like to play with Ricky because he wasn't a very good player.

Activity 20- Tommy's Little Brother

Student:________________________________   Date:______________

Tommy liked to play football. He played football with his friends almost every day. His little brother, Ricky, always wanted to play with him. Ricky loved football but could not catch the ball. Tommy didn't like to play with Ricky because he wasn't a very good player.

1. How do you think Ricky felt when his big brother didn't want to play with him?

   ____

   ____

   ____

2. Should Tommy be patient and try to help Ricky play better?

   ____

   ____

   ____

3. How would Tommy feel if his parents made him play with Ricky?

   ____

   ____

   ____

4. How would Ricky feel if his big brother helped him learn to play better?

   ____

   ____

   ____

5. How do you think Tommy's friends would feel about letting Ricky play with them?

____

____

____

6. Have you ever wanted to play with someone who didn't want to play with you? How did you feel?

____

____

____

Paulo's Haircut

Paulo came to school one day with a new haircut. His
friend, Joey, laughed at him because of his funny new
haircut and called him names. Others joined in the teasing.
Paulo felt silly and ran away.

Activity 21- Paulo's Haircut

Student:________________________________   Date:_______________

Paulo came to school one day with a new haircut. His friend, Joey, laughed at him because of his funny new haircut and called him names. Others joined in the teasing. Paulo felt silly and ran away.

1. Why did Paulo feel bad?

____

____

____

2. Why do you think Joey laughed at Paulo?

____

____

____

3. How do you think you would have felt if you were Paulo?

____

____

____

4. What would you have said to Joey and the others?

____

____

____

5. What would you say to Paulo if you didn't like his haircut?

____

____

____

6. How would Paulo feel if he really liked his new haircut and his friends kept laughing at him?

____

____

____

Lilly's Family

Lilly's family came to the United States from Japan. In Japan, people take off their shoes before coming into a house. They also eat many foods that people in other countries don't even know about.

When Kevin went to play at Lilly's house, he was asked to take off his shoes before coming inside. Kevin thought this was strange, but he did it anyway.

Later, Lilly's mom brought them a snack. Kevin had never eaten anything like this, but tried it anyway. To his surprise he liked it. Kevin decided that it was fun trying new things!

Activity 22- Lilly's Family

Student:_________________________________   Date:_______________

Lilly's family came to the United States from Japan. In Japan, people take off their shoes before coming into a house. They also eat many foods that people in other countries don't even know about.

When Kevin went to play at Lilly's house, he was asked to take off his shoes before coming inside. Kevin thought this was strange, but he did it anyway.

Later, Lilly's mom brought them a snack. Kevin had never eaten anything like this, but tried it anyway. To his surprise he liked it. Kevin decided that it was fun trying new things!

1. How did Kevin feel about doing things in a different way at Lilly's home?

   ____

   ____

   ____

2. How do you think Lilly felt about being different?

   ____

   ____

   ____

3. How do you think Lilly and her family felt about Kevin being different from them?

   ____

   ____

   ____

4. Do you think Kevin will feel strange next time he goes to Lilly's house? Why?

____

____

____

5. Have you ever had a friend who came from a different country? How was this person different from you and your other friends?

____

____

____

6. How do you feel about people who are different from you in many ways?

____

____

____

The Broken Vase

Janet was playing at her friend Helen's house. Helen had a beautiful new vase near the window. Janet picked up the vase to look at how it sparkled in the sunlight. Then it slipped out of her fingers. The vase hit the floor with a big crash. Helen's mom yelled at her and told her to go home.

Activity 23- The Broken Vase

Janet was playing at her friend Helen's house. Helen had a beautiful new vase near the window. Janet picked up the vase to look at how it sparkled in the sunlight. Then it slipped out of her fingers. The vase hit the floor with a big crash. Helen's mom yelled at Janet and told her to go home.

1. How do you think Janet felt when she saw the beautiful vase?

    ____

    ____

    ____

2. How do you think Janet felt about breaking the vase?

    ____

    ____

    ____

3. How do you think Helen felt when her mom yelled at Janet?

    ____

    ____

    ____

4. How do you think Helen's mom felt about the broken vase?

    ____

    ____

    ____

5. Should Janet tell her parents about what happened?

____

____

____

6. Do you think Janet and Helen should still be friends?

____

____

____

The White Dress

Cindy had a pretty new white dress. At lunch time, she dropped a cup of juice. It spilled all over her dress. The juice made a big stain. She tried to wash out the stain, but it wouldn't come out. Cindy worried that her mom would get mad at her, so she hid the dress.

Activity 24- The White Dress

Student:_________________________________   Date:______________

Cindy had a pretty new white dress. At lunch time, she dropped a cup of juice. It spilled all over her dress. The juice made a big stain. She tried to wash out the stain, but it wouldn't come out. Cindy worried that her mom would get mad at her, so she hid the dress.

1. How did Cindy feel about her pretty new dress?

   ____

   ____

   ____

2. How did Cindy feel about ruining her dress?

   ____

   ____

   ____

3. What do you think Cindy's mom would do if she found out that Cindy had spilled juice on the dress?

   ____

   ____

   ____

4. How would Cindy feel if she told her mom what happened and asked for help cleaning the dress?

   ____

   ____

   ____

5. How would Cindy's mother feel if she knew that Cindy hid the dress?

____

76

____

____

6. Has anything like this ever happened to you? How did you feel?

____

____

____

The Favorite Doll

Mary and Alexis were good friends. Mary always let Alexis play with her toys. One day, Mary went to visit Alexis to play. Alexis was playing with her favorite doll. Mary asked if she could play with the doll, but Alexis was afraid that she might break it.

Activity 25- The Favorite Doll

Student:_________________________________   Date:______________

Mary and Alexis were good friends. Mary always let Alexis play with her toys. One day, Mary went to visit Alexis to play. Alexis was playing with her favorite doll. Mary asked if she could play with the doll, but Alexis was afraid that she might break it.

1. Why do you think Mary and Alexis were such good friends?

____

____

____

2. Should Alexis let Mary play with the doll?

____

____

____

3. Should Alexis keep playing with the doll if she doesn't want to let Mary play with it?

____

____

____

4. How would Mary feel if Alexis told her that she couldn't play with her doll?

____

____

____

5. Have you ever had a favorite toy that you didn't want to share with anyone else? What would you do if someone wanted to play with it?

____

____

____

6. Has anyone ever said that you couldn't play with one of his or her toys? How did that make you feel about your friend?

____

____

____

7. How do you feel when you share your toys with a friend?

____

____

____

Jimmy's Messy Room

Jimmy let his friends come to his house after school.
They played with toy cars in his room and had a lot of fun.
His friends made a big mess. They didn't clean up the mess
before leaving. Jimmy was afraid that his parents would be
mad about the mess.

Activity 26- Jimmy's Messy Room

Student:_________________________________ Date:_______________

Jimmy let his friends come to his house after school. They played with toy cars in his room and had a lot of fun. His friends made a big mess. They didn't clean up the mess before leaving. Jimmy was afraid that his parents would be mad about the mess.

1. Should Jimmy clean up the mess in his room before his parents see it?

____

____

____

2. How do you think Jimmy felt when his friends left without cleaning up?

____

____

____

3. Should Jimmy find his friends and ask them to help pick up the mess?

____

____

____

4. How would Jimmy's friends feel if he got punished for the mess? Why?

____

____

____

5. Should Jimmy invite his friends over to play again?

____

____

____

6. Should Jimmy go to visit his friends and make a mess in their rooms?

____

____

____

Horseback Riding

Veronica and Ashley were sisters. Their mother told them that they could go horseback riding if they were good and did all of their chores. They were very excited because they liked horses.

They finished all of their chores. Then they started to argue. Their mother got mad at them for arguing and said, "I'm not taking you horseback riding because you are being too bad."

Activity 27- Horseback Riding

Student:________________________________   Date:______________

Veronica and Ashley were sisters. Their mother told them that they could go horseback riding if they were good and did all of their chores. They were very excited because they liked horses.

They finished all of their chores. Then they started to argue. Their mother got mad at them for arguing and said, "I'm not taking you horseback riding because you are being too bad."

1. How did Veronica and Ashley feel about going horseback riding?

____

____

____

2. How did Veronica and Ashley feel when their mother said they were too bad to go horseback riding?

____

____

____

3. Should they argue with their mother and beg her to take them horseback riding?

____

____

____

4. Should they blame each other for upsetting their mother?

____

____

____

5. How do you think their mother felt when she told them they couldn't go
horseback riding?

____

____

____

6. Do you ever argue with someone when you know it is best not to argue?
How do you feel after the argument?

____

____

____

The Baseball Card

Jeffrey and his friend, Bo, collected baseball cards. Bo really wanted to trade for one of Jeffrey's cards, but Jeffrey didn't want to give it away. The card had a picture of Bo's favorite baseball player on it. After Bo left, Jeffrey noticed that the card was missing.

Activity 28- The Baseball Card

Student:_________________________________ Date:______________

Jeffrey and his friend, Bo, collected baseball cards. Bo really wanted to trade for one of Jeffrey's cards, but Jeffrey didn't want to give it away. The card had a picture of Bo's favorite baseball player on it. After Bo left, Jeffrey noticed that the card was missing.

1. How do you think Bo felt when he found out that Jeffrey had a card that he really wanted?

____

____

____

2. How do you think Bo felt when Jeffrey wouldn't trade the card to him?

____

____

____

3. How do you think Jeffrey felt about the missing card?

____

____

____

4. Should Jeffrey blame Bo for taking the card? Why?

____

____

____

5. How do you think Bo would feel if Jeffrey blamed him for stealing the card when he hadn't really stolen it?

____

____

____

6. What do you think Jeffrey should do to find out where the missing card is?

____

____

____

7. Have you ever had anything stolen from you? How did it make you feel?

____

____

____

Jennie's Art

Jennie was a good artist. Her favorite time in school was when she did art projects. She liked when her teacher told her that her drawings were excellent. Most of Jennie's classmates liked her art. Jennie would draw pictures for them.

Ruby wanted to be a good artist like Jennie. She never told Jennie that she thought she was a good artist. She always said mean things. "Your pictures look stupid," said Ruby.

Jennie's feelings were hurt. She was confused because everyone else liked her drawings.

Activity 29- Jennie's Art

Student:_________________________________ Date:______________

Jennie was a good artist. Her favorite time in school was when she did art projects. She liked when her teacher told her that her drawings were excellent. Most of Jennie's classmates liked her art. Jennie would draw pictures for them.

Ruby wanted to be a good artist like Jennie. She never told Jennie that she thought she was a good artist. She always said mean things. "Your pictures look stupid," said Ruby.

Jennie's feelings were hurt. She was confused because everyone else liked her drawings.

1. How did Jennie feel about being a good artist?

____

____

____

2. How did Jennie feel when she shared her art with her friends?

____

____

____

3. Why do you think Ruby was so mean to Jennie?

____

____

____

4. What could you say to Jennie to help her feel better?

____

____

____

5. What would you say to Ruby?

____

____

____

6. What special things can you do that you are proud of?

____

____

____

7. How does it make you feel when others tell you that you do something very well?

____

____

____

The Dog Watcher

Sheila was watching her neighbor's dog, Wally, while they were out of town on vacation. Sheila took good care of Wally. She made sure he had food and water and took him for walks every day. One day Sheila forgot to close the gate and Wally ran away.

Sheila looked and looked for Wally, but couldn't find him anywhere. A few days later, Wally came back home. He was dirty and tired, but safe. Sheila cleaned him up just in time for his owners to get back.

Activity 30- The Dog Watcher

Student:_________________________________   Date:_______________

Sheila was watching her neighbor's dog, Wally, while they were out of town on vacation. Sheila took good care of Wally. She made sure he had food and water and took him for walks every day. One day Sheila forgot to close the gate and Wally ran away.

Sheila looked and looked for Wally, but couldn't find him anywhere. A few days later, Wally came back home. He was dirty and tired, but safe. Sheila cleaned him up just in time for his owners to get back.

1. How did Sheila feel about Wally before he ran away?

____

____

____

2. How do you think the neighbors felt about Sheila when they let her care for Wally? Why?

____

____

____

3. How did Sheila feel when Wally ran away?

____

____

____

4. How would Wally's owners feel if they knew he was lost?

____

____

____

5. How did Sheila feel when Wally came back?

____

____

____

6. How would you feel if the dog you were taking care of ran away?

____

____

____

Part 2

Feeling Comparison Worksheets

Each of the worksheets in this section includes activities related to two feelings that are opposites. The worksheets can be used to stimulate discussions about common feelings experienced by students. They can also be used to expand children's vocabulary by teaching words related in meaning or often associated with specific feelings. The worksheets may be reproduced for use with individual students.

Activity 1- Happy and Sad

Student:______________________________   Date:______________

A. Feeling Happy and Feeling Sad

Instructions: Think of some things that make you feel happy. Then think of some things that make you feel sad. Let's write them all down on this list.

Happy	Sad
______________________	______________________
______________________	______________________
______________________	______________________
______________________	______________________
______________________	______________________
______________________	______________________
______________________	______________________
______________________	______________________

B. Feeling Words

Instructions: Some of the words in this list are used when someone is feeling happy and some are used when someone is feeling sad. Let's see if you can find the words that go with "happy" and the words that go with "sad."

	Happy	Sad
joyful	____	____
moody	____	____
cheerful	____	____
glad	____	____
grumpy	____	____
miserable	____	____
delighted	____	____
depressed	____	____

C. Sharing Our Feelings- Happy or Sad

Instructions: Tell a story about a time when you felt happy or sad. Talk about why you felt the way you did.

____

____

____

____

____

____

____

____

____

Now ask a friend to tell you how he or she would have felt in the same situation. What did your friend say?

____

____

____

____

Activity 2- Brave and Afraid

Student:_______________________________   Date:_______________

A. Feeling Brave and Feeling Afraid

Instructions: Think of some things that make you feel brave. Then think of some things that make you feel afraid. Let's write them all down on this list.

Brave   **Afraid**

_________________________   _________________________

_________________________   _________________________

_________________________   _________________________

_________________________   _________________________

_________________________   _________________________

_________________________   _________________________

_________________________   _________________________

_________________________   _________________________

B. Feeling Words

Instructions: Some of the words in this list are used when we feel brave and some are used when we feel afraid. Let's see if you can find the words that go with "brave" and the words that go with "afraid."

	Brave	**Afraid**
scared	____	____
nervous	____	____
courageous	____	____
frightened	____	____
fearful	____	____
terrified	____	____
bold	____	____
confident	____	____

C. Sharing Our Feelings - Brave or Afraid

Instructions: Tell a story about a time when you felt brave or afraid. Talk about why you felt the way you did.

____

____

____

____

____

____

____

____

____

Now ask a friend to tell you how he or she would have felt in the same situation. What did your friend say?

____

____

____

____

Activity 3- Calm and Upset

Student:_________________________________ Date:_______________

A. Feeling Calm and Feeling Upset

Instructions: Think of some things that make you feel calm. Then think of some things that make you feel upset. Let's write them all down on this list.

Calm   **Upset**

_______________________________________   _______________________________________

_______________________________________   _______________________________________

_______________________________________   _______________________________________

_______________________________________   _______________________________________

_______________________________________   _______________________________________

_______________________________________   _______________________________________

_______________________________________   _______________________________________

B. Feeling Words

Instructions: Some of the words in this list are used when we feel calm and some are used when we feel upset. Let's see if you can find the words that go with "calm" and the words that go with "upset."

	Calm	Upset
relaxed	____	____
angry	____	____
quiet	____	____
rested	____	____
mad	____	____
annoyed	____	____
peaceful	____	____
furious	____	____

C. Sharing Our Feelings - Calm or Upset

Instructions: Tell a story about a time when you felt calm or upset. Talk about why you felt the way you did.

____

____

____

____

____

____

____

____

____

Now ask a friend to tell you how he or she would have felt in the same situation. What did your friend say?

____

____

____

____

Activity 4- Friendly and Mean

Student:_______________________________   Date:______________

A. Acting Friendly and Acting Mean

Instructions: Think of some things people do when they are acting friendly. Then think of some things people do when they are acting mean. Let's write them all down on this list.

Friendly   **Mean**

___________________________   ___________________________

___________________________   ___________________________

___________________________   ___________________________

___________________________   ___________________________

___________________________   ___________________________

___________________________   ___________________________

___________________________   ___________________________

B. Feeling Words

Instructions: Some of the words in this list are used when someone is acting friendly and some are used when someone is acting mean. Let's see if you can find the words that go with "friendly" and the words that go with "mean."

	Friendly	Mean
nasty	___	___
cruel	___	___
helpful	___	___
likeable	___	___
hostile	___	___
bossy	___	___
pleasant	___	___
agreeable	___	___

C. Sharing Our Feelings - Friendly or Mean

Instructions: Tell a story about a time when you were feeling friendly or feeling mean. Talk about why you felt the way you did.

____

____

____

____

____

____

____

____

____

Now ask a friend to tell you how he or she would have felt in the same situation. What did your friend say?

____

____

____

____

Activity 5- Tired and Energetic

Student:_________________________________   Date:_______________

A. Feeling Tired or Feeling Energetic

Instructions: Think of some things people do when they are feeling tired. Then think of some things people do when they are feeling energetic. Let's write them all down on this list.

Tired   **Energetic**

____

____

____

____

____

____

B. Feeling Words

Instructions: Some of the words in this list are used when someone is feeling tired and some are used when someone is feeling energetic. Let's see if you can find the words that go with "tired" and the words that go with "energetic."

	Tired	Energetic
strong	____	____
fresh	____	____
exhausted	____	____
bushed	____	____
sleepy	____	____
lively	____	____
active	____	____
strained	____	____

C. Sharing Our Feelings - Tired or Energetic

Instructions: Tell a story about a time when you were feeling tired or energetic. Talk about why you felt the way you did.

____

____

____

____

____

____

____

____

____

Now ask a friend to tell you how he or she would have felt in the same situation. What did your friend say?

____

____

____

____

Activity 6- Proud and Ashamed

Student:_________________________________   Date:_______________

A. Feeling Proud or Feeling Ashamed

Instructions: Think of some things people do that make them feel proud. Then think of some things people do that make them feel ashamed. Let's write them all down on this list.

Proud   **Ashamed**

______________________   ______________________

______________________   ______________________

______________________   ______________________

______________________   ______________________

______________________   ______________________

______________________   ______________________

B. Feeling Words

Instructions: Some of the words in this list are used when someone is feeling proud and some are used when someone is feeling ashamed. Let's see if you can find the words that go with "proud" and the words that go with "ashamed."

	Proud	Ashamed
embarrassed	____	____
honored	____	____
pleased	____	____
disappointed	____	____
sorry	____	____
delighted	____	____
happy	____	____
dishonored	____	____

C. Sharing Our Feelings - Proud or Ashamed

Instructions: Tell a story about a time when you were feeling proud or ashamed
of something. Talk about why you felt the way you did.

____

____

____

____

____

____

____

____

____

Now ask a friend to tell you how he or she would have felt in the same situation.
What did your friend say?

____

____

____

____

Activity 7- Love and Hate

Student:_________________________________   Date:_______________

A. Feeling Love or Feeling Hate

Instructions: Think of some things that cause people to feel loved. Then think of some things that cause people to feel hated. Let's write them all down on this list.

Love   **Hate**

_________________________   _________________________

_________________________   _________________________

_________________________   _________________________

_________________________   _________________________

_________________________   _________________________

_________________________   _________________________

_________________________   _________________________

B. Feeling Words

Instructions: Some of the words in this list are used when someone feels loving and some are used when someone feels hateful. Let's see if you can find the words that go with "love" and the words that go with "hate."

	Love	Hate
affectionate	__	__
warm	__	__
cold	__	__
caring	__	__
unfriendly	__	__
heartless	__	__
cruel	__	__
friendly	__	__

C. Sharing Our Feelings - Love or Hate

Instructions: Tell a story about a time when you felt loved or you felt hated. Talk about why you felt the way you did.

____

____

____

____

____

____

____

____

____

Now ask a friend to tell you how he or she would have felt in the same situation. What did your friend say?

____

____

____

____

Activity 8- Healthy and Sick

Student:_______________________________   Date:_______________

A. Feeling Healthy or Feeling Sick

Instructions: Think of some things that cause people to feel healthy. Then think of some things that cause people to feel sick. Let's write them all down on this list.

Healthy   **Sick**

_______________________   _______________________

_______________________   _______________________

_______________________   _______________________

_______________________   _______________________

_______________________   _______________________

_______________________   _______________________

B. Feeling Words

Instructions: Some of the words in this list are used when someone feels healthy and some are used when someone feels sick. Let's see if you can find the words that go with "healthy" and the words that go with "sick."

	Healthy	Sick
energetic	____	____
strong	____	____
depressed	____	____
ill	____	____
weak	____	____
tired	____	____
well	____	____
fit	____	____

C. Sharing Our Feelings - Healthy or Sick

Instructions: Tell a story about a time when you felt healthy or you felt sick. Talk about why you felt the way you did.

____

____

____

____

____

____

____

____

____

Now ask a friend to tell you how he or she would have felt in the same situation. What did your friend say?

____

____

____

____

Activity 9- Guess the Feeling

Student:_________________________________ Date:_______________

Instructions: Guess the feeling that is missing from each of these sentences.

1. Cheryl yelled at her brother. Cheryl was _________________.

2. Brian laughed at Shelley's joke. Brian was _________________.

3. Corel cried when the thunder was loud. Corel was _________________.

4. Janet smiled when David gave her a hug. Janet was _________________.

5. Carmella hid when the big dog growled at her. Carmella was _________________.

6. Luke complained when dinner was late. Luke was _________________.

7. Manuel snapped at his sister when she woke him up. Manuel was _________________.

8. Joseph pouted when no one would play with him. Joseph was _________________.

9. Harry caught a big, scary spider. Harry was _________________.

10. Raymond grabbed the toy from Sally. Raymond was _________________.

11. Annie won a special award. Annie was _________________.

12. Fernando listened to the soft music. Fernando was _________________.

13. Rose wanted to run around and play outside. Rose was _________________.

14. Albert tripped and fell in front of his classmates. Albert was _________________.

15. Marina was in a bad mood and didn't want to play.
Marina was _______________.

16. Clark lost his pet turtle. Clark was _______________.

17. Larry got straight A's on his report card. Larry was _______________.

18. Vanessa had many friends. Vanessa was _______________.

19. Sherman's mom gave him a big hug. Sherman was _______________.

20. Sam slammed his door when he was punished. Sam was _______________.

21. Bonnie received a birthday card in the mail. Bonnie was _______________.

22. Anthony didn't want to clean his room. Anthony was _______________.

23. Joey saw his friend playing with another boy. Joey was _______________.

24. Charlotte cried when she couldn't have her way.
Charlotte was _______________.

25. Buddy didn't feel well and missed the class field trip. Buddy
was _______________.

26. Mike told the bully to stop picking on his little sister.
Mike was _______________.

27. Harold ran away from the monster in his dream. Harold was _______________.

28. Ben was chosen to give a speech to his class. Ben was _______________.

29. Rebecca laid in the hammock under a tree. Rebecca was _______________.

30. Ken stayed up late doing his homework. Ken was _______________.

Part 3

Drawing Feelings

Three drawing activities are included for each of the 13 feelings in this section. Children, for example, draw three pictures for the feeling "happy."

1. Imagine that you are happy. Draw doodles about this feeling.
2. Draw something that makes you feel happy.
3. Draw yourself when you are happy.

After children have drawn their pictures, ask them to talk about the feelings shown in the pictures. Students, for example, might be asked to draw pictures showing "friendly" and pictures showing "mean." After completing their drawings, students can discuss how these two feelings are related and how these two feelings have been experienced in various situations at school and at home.

When children are asked to draw pictures showing a negative feeling such as "mean," it is important for them to understand that it is normal to experience both negative and positive feelings. When negative feelings are discussed, always give students an opportunity to draw a positive feeling during the same lesson. By providing opportunities for students to compare different feelings, they will experience greater benefits from the instructional activities.

Worksheets are included in this section for drawing 13 specific feelings. The "blank" worksheets on pages 155-157 can be used to present any additional feelings that teachers wish to include in the drawing activities. All of the worksheets in this section may be reproduced for use with individual students.

HAPPY

Imagine you are happy. Draw doodles about this feeling.

HAPPY

Draw something that makes you feel happy.

Name:_____________________________   Date:_____________

HAPPY

Draw yourself when you are happy.

SAD

Imagine you are sad. Draw doodles about this feeling.

SAD

Draw something that makes you feel sad.

SAD

Draw yourself when you are sad.

CALM

Imagine you are calm. Draw doodles about this feeling.

Name:______________________   Date:_____________

CALM

Draw something that makes you feel calm.

CALM

Draw yourself when you are calm.

UPSET

Imagine you are upset. Draw doodles about this feeling.

UPSET

Draw something that makes you upset.

Name:___________________________   Date:_______________

UPSET

Draw yourself when you are upset.

FRIENDLY

Imagine you are friendly. Draw doodles showing this feeling.

FRIENDLY

Draw something that makes you feel friendly.

FRIENDLY

Draw yourself when you are friendly.

Name:____________________   Date:____________

MEAN

Imagine you are mean. Draw doodles showing this feeling.

MEAN

Draw something that makes you feel mean.

MEAN

Draw yourself when you are mean.

Name:________________________   Date:____________

TIRED

Imagine you are tired. Draw doodles showing this feeling.

TIRED

Draw something that makes you feel tired.

TIRED

Draw yourself when you are tired.

ENERGETIC

Imagine you are energetic. Draw doodles showing this feeling.

Name:_____________________   Date:____________

Copyright © 1992 by Academic Communication Associates. This page may be reproduced.

ENERGETIC

Draw something that makes you feel energetic.

ENERGETIC

Draw yourself when you are energetic.

Name:_______________________   Date:____________

LOVE

Imagine you are loving. Draw doodles showing this feeling.

Name:________________________   Date:____________

LOVE

Draw something that makes you feel loving.

LOVE

Draw yourself when you are loving.

HATE

Imagine you are feeling hateful. Draw doodles showing this feeling.

Name:_______________________   Date:______________

HATE

Draw something that makes you feel hateful.

HATE

Draw yourself when you are feeling hateful.

Name:______________________________   Date:_______________

PROUD

Imagine you are proud. Draw doodles showing this feeling.

Name:_____________________   Date:____________

PROUD

Draw something that makes you feel proud.

PROUD

Draw yourself when you are proud.

ASHAMED

Imagine you are ashamed. Draw doodles showing this feeling.

Name:______________________________   Date:______________

ASHAMED

Draw something that makes you feel ashamed.

ASHAMED

Draw yourself when you are ashamed.

LONELY

Imagine you are lonely. Draw doodles showing this feeling.

LONELY

Draw something that makes you feel lonely.

LONELY

Draw yourself when you are lonely.

Write the name of a feeling.

____

Draw doodles showing this feeling.

Name:_________________________   Date:______________

Write the name of a feeling.

____

Draw something that makes you feel this way.

Name:____________________________   Date:______________

Write the name of a feeling.

____

Draw yourself when you are feeling this way.